RORY MCILROY: THE GOLF STAR KID!

A Fun-Filled Exploration of Golf's Youngest Champion

Johnny Samuel

Copyright © 2024 by Johnny Samuel

All rights reserved. No part of this publication may be reproduced, stored in a retrieval system, or transmitted in any form or by any means, electronic, mechanical, photocopying, recording, or scanning, without the prior written permission of the publisher.

The information provided in this book is for general informational purposes only. The author and publisher make no representation or warranties concerning the accuracy, applicability, or completeness of the contents.

The author and publisher shall not be held liable for any loss or damages arising from the use of this book.

TABLE OF CONTENT

INTRODUCTION
Rory McIlroy: The Golf Star Kid!

CHAPTER 1
A Star is Born: Rory McIlroy's Arrival

CHAPTER 2
Swinging into Action: How Rory Discovered His Love for Golf

CHAPTER 3
Family First: Meet the Supportive Team Behind Rory

CHAPTER 4
Growing Up Big Dreams: Rory's Path to Greatness

CHAPTER 5
The Big Win: Rory's First Major Championship Victory

CHAPTER
Words of Wisdom: Inspiring Quotes from Rory McIlroy

CHAPTER 7
Golf Fun: Rory's Best Tips and Tricks for Young Players

CHAPTER 8
Around the Globe: Rory's Adventures on the Golf Course

CHAPTER 9
Facing Challenges: Rory's Comebacks and Valuable Lessons

CHAPTER 10
Dream Big: How You Can Follow in Rory's Footsteps!

CONCLUSION
Rory's Amazing Journey!

INTRODUCTION

Rory McIlroy: The Golf Star Kid!

Welcome to the exciting journey of Rory McIlroy, a kid who turned his passion for golf into a grand adventure! Picture a young boy dreaming of playing in big tournaments and one day becoming a superstar. That's exactly what Rory did!

From a young age, Rory showed incredible talent. With every practice, he got closer to his dreams. But it wasn't always easy. Like many kids, he faced challenges and learned important lessons about hard work, determination, and never giving up. This book will take you through Rory's amazing story, showing you how he turned dreams into reality.

As you explore these pages, you'll discover the fun and excitement of golf through Rory's eyes. You'll cheer for him as he navigates ups and downs and learn that it's okay to stumble along the way. Each chapter is packed with inspiration, teaching you that with passion and perseverance, you can reach for the stars, just like Rory.

So, are you ready to enter the world of golf with Rory McIlroy? Let's embark on this thrilling adventure together, where you'll see how a young boy's dreams became a shining reality! Get ready for fun, inspiration, and all the excitement that comes with being a golf star!

CHAPTER 1

A Star is Born: Rory McIlroy's Arrival on May 4, 1989

Once upon a time, in a cozy little town called Holywood in Northern Ireland, a star was born! On May 4, 1989, Rory McIlroy entered the world. From the very beginning, it was clear that he was destined for something special. But like all great stories, this one starts with a little boy who had big dreams.

Rory was the only child of Gerry and Rosie McIlroy. His parents loved sports, especially golf, and they passed that passion onto their son. While many babies play with rattles, Rory was often seen with a miniature golf club! His parents quickly realized that he was not just any ordinary kid; he had a unique spark in his eyes whenever he saw a golf ball.

Growing up, Rory was surrounded by beautiful green fields and golf courses. He would often go to the local club with his dad. Picture a small boy, giggling with excitement, as he took his first swing. Though his shots were sometimes wobbly, each swing was filled with joy and determination. The golf course became his playground, and the game began to feel like magic.

As he got older, Rory practiced a lot. He would spend hours hitting balls, dreaming of becoming a famous golfer one day. His family supported him every step of the way. They encouraged him to keep trying, even when things got tough. Rory's dad taught him that every great player has to start somewhere, and every swing brings him closer to his dreams.

Rory didn't just play golf; he watched it too! He admired famous golfers like Tiger Woods and always dreamed of being like them. With every match he watched on TV, he soaked in tips and tricks. He would shout at the screen, cheering for his heroes, imagining himself in their shoes. This made him practice even harder!

But Rory's journey wasn't all about sunshine and rainbows. Like many kids, he faced challenges. There were days when he missed the ball or when he felt like giving up. However, each time he stumbled, his family reminded him of how important it was to keep trying. They taught him that mistakes are just stepping stones to success. This lesson stuck with him, and it became a part of who he was.

When he was just a teenager, Rory entered his first golf tournament. Imagine a young boy, heart racing, standing in front of a crowd! He felt nervous but excited. With his family cheering him on, Rory gave it his all. He didn't win that tournament, but it didn't matter. He loved every moment, and the thrill of competition only fueled his passion more.

By the time he turned 16, Rory was no longer just a kid with a dream; he was a rising star in the golf world! He became the youngest player ever to win the U.S. Amateur Championship. Can you imagine how proud his parents felt? They watched their son shine on the big stage, knowing that all those hours of practice were paying off.

As Rory continued to grow, so did his talent. He turned professional at the age of 18, and just like that, he was on his way to becoming one of the best golfers in the world. With every swing of his club, he inspired countless kids to chase their dreams. Rory showed them that with hard work and determination, anything is possible.

Rory's story reminds us that every star has a beginning. Whether it's a little boy swinging a golf club in a backyard or a young girl dreaming of becoming an astronaut, we all have our own paths to follow. The key is to believe in ourselves and never give up, just like Rory did.

So, the next time you see someone practicing their sport or working hard on their dreams, remember that they, too, are on their journey to greatness. Just like Rory McIlroy, who started as a small boy with big dreams, we all have the power to shine bright in our own special way!

And that, dear readers, is how Rory McIlroy came into the world—a little boy with a love for golf who would go on to inspire millions!

CHAPTER 2

Swinging into Action: How Rory Discovered His Love for Golf

Every great adventure begins with a single step, and for Rory McIlroy, that step was taken when he was just a little boy. Picture a sunny day in Holywood, Northern Ireland, where the grass was as green as a freshly mowed lawn. Little Rory, barely three years old, was about to discover a passion that would change his life forever.

It all started when Rory's dad, Gerry, decided to take him to a nearby golf course. Gerry was a big fan of golf and often played with his friends. One day, he thought, "Why not bring my son along?" So, they packed a small bag with a few golf balls and a tiny club that looked almost like a toy. As they arrived at the course, Rory's eyes sparkled with excitement. He had never seen such a vast, beautiful place!

When they stepped onto the green, something magical happened. Rory watched as his dad swung his club, sending the ball soaring through the air. It was a sight to behold! With every swing, the ball danced across the grass, and Rory couldn't help but giggle. He wanted to try! So, with a little help from his dad, Rory picked up the club and took his first swing. Although the ball barely rolled, the joy on his face was unforgettable.

From that moment on, golf became Rory's favorite game. He was fascinated by the way the club felt in his hands and the thrill of watching the ball fly. His dad encouraged him, teaching him the basics, like how to hold the club and how to stand. With each lesson, Rory's excitement grew. He was determined to improve, and practice became his best friend.

Rory spent every possible moment at the golf course. While other kids played soccer or rode bikes, he was out on the green, practicing his swings. He would challenge himself to hit the ball further each time, imagining himself as a great golfer like his heroes. Watching the professionals on TV only fueled his desire to play better. Rory learned from their techniques and began to dream big.

But it wasn't all smooth sailing. Just like any young athlete, Rory faced his share of challenges. There were days when the ball wouldn't go where he wanted, and frustration crept in. He felt like giving up at times. Yet, with the support of his family, especially his dad, he learned that every golfer faces ups and downs. They reminded him that even the best players started out just like him—full of mistakes but eager to learn.

At age seven, Rory joined a local golf club. This was an exciting step! He made new friends who shared his love for the game. They practiced together, laughed together, and sometimes even played little competitions. Rory loved the feeling of camaraderie and friendly rivalry. It made the game even more enjoyable. They would often talk about their favorite golfers and mimic their swings, turning the golf course into a playground filled with dreams.

One sunny day, Rory's club held a junior tournament. Imagine the buzz of excitement as kids gathered, each hoping to showcase their skills! Rory felt a mix of nerves and exhilaration. This was his chance to show

how much he had learned. As he stood on the first tee, he could feel his heart racing. He took a deep breath, remembered his practice, and swung the club. The ball soared, and cheers erupted from his friends and family. That moment ignited a fire within him, fueling his passion even more.

As Rory continued to grow, so did his talent. He entered more tournaments, and each time he played, he learned something new. Sometimes he won, and sometimes he didn't, but each experience taught him about resilience, sportsmanship, and the importance of having fun. Rory began to understand that golf wasn't just about winning; it was about enjoying the game and celebrating the friendships he built along the way.

His love for golf wasn't just about playing; it was also about exploring the beauty of nature. Rory loved spending time outdoors, surrounded by tall trees, colorful flowers, and the gentle sound of the wind. The golf course felt like a magical kingdom where he could escape and be himself. This connection to nature made him appreciate the game even more.

As he entered his teenage years, Rory began to realize that he had a special talent. He was hitting the ball farther and with more accuracy. Coaches took notice, and soon he was invited to play in more prestigious tournaments. Each new opportunity was a stepping stone, bringing him closer to his dreams.

Rory's journey wasn't just about personal achievements; he also wanted to inspire others. He remembered how much joy golf brought him and wanted to share that joy with kids everywhere. He began to dream of one day becoming a professional golfer, not just for the trophies but to show other children that they, too, could follow their passions and achieve greatness.

Through hard work, determination, and the unwavering support of his family, Rory's love for golf blossomed. Every swing was a celebration, and every game was an adventure. As he stood on the course, he knew he was on the right path. Golf had taught him lessons that would last a lifetime: the value of perseverance, the importance of friendships, and the joy of following your dreams.

And so, from that sunny day when a little boy picked up a golf club, Rory McIlroy began his incredible journey—a journey filled with laughter, challenges, and endless swings. This was just the beginning of a story that would inspire countless young golfers around the world.

CHAPTER 3

Family First: Meet the Supportive Team Behind Rory

Every great athlete has a team cheering them on, and for Rory McIlroy, that team was his family. Growing up in Holywood, Northern Ireland, Rory was surrounded by love and encouragement, which played a huge role in shaping him into the champion golfer he would become.

Rory's parents, Gerry and Rosie, were his biggest fans from day one. Gerry, a golf enthusiast, not only introduced Rory to the game but also instilled a passion for sports in him. He would often take Rory to the golf course, where they spent countless hours together. Imagine a young boy laughing as his dad showed him how to swing a club, and you can picture the special bond they shared. Gerry believed in Rory's talent, always encouraging him to aim high and work hard.

Rosie, on the other hand, was the glue that held the family together. She was Rory's biggest supporter off the course. Whether it was helping him with schoolwork or cheering him on during tournaments, Rosie was always there. She knew how important it was for Rory to balance his love for golf with his studies. She often reminded him that education was just as important as sports, helping him manage his time wisely. This support allowed Rory to focus on his game without neglecting his responsibilities.

Rory's family didn't just support him financially; they supported him emotionally too. They celebrated his victories with hugs and high-fives, and when things didn't go as planned, they were there to lift his spirits. Rory learned early on that winning wasn't everything; what mattered most was having fun and enjoying the game. This positive attitude became a key part of his personality and helped him through tough times.

As Rory grew older, his family continued to play a vital role in his development as a golfer. They traveled with him to tournaments, creating unforgettable memories along the way. Imagine the excitement of road trips, packed with snacks, laughter, and dreams of future victories. These trips brought them closer together and made Rory feel like he had a whole cheering squad behind him.

One of the most memorable moments for Rory was when he competed in his first big tournament. It was a nerve-wracking experience for any young athlete, but with his parents by his side, he felt ready to take on the challenge. They helped calm his nerves and reminded him to enjoy every moment.

And when Rory stepped onto the green, he could hear their cheers ringing in his ears, giving him the confidence to shine.

But it wasn't just his parents who were part of his support team. Rory also had extended family who encouraged him in his journey. His grandparents and uncles would attend his matches, waving flags and holding signs that read "Go Rory!" Their pride in his accomplishments filled his heart with joy and made him feel even more determined to succeed.

In addition to family, Rory had coaches who became like family members too. They taught him not just the skills of the game, but also life lessons about dedication, discipline, and resilience. They pushed him to work hard, but they also celebrated every improvement, no matter how small. This nurturing environment helped Rory grow into a confident and skilled golfer.

Rory often reflects on how crucial his family's support has been in his life. He knows that he wouldn't be where he is today without their love and encouragement. It's a reminder to all of us that having a strong support system can make all the difference in achieving our dreams.

As Rory began to make a name for himself in the golfing world, he never forgot where he came from. He often credits his family for his success, and he remains grounded despite the fame and accolades. He understands the importance of giving back, and he often involves his family in charitable activities. Whether it's raising funds for children's hospitals or supporting youth sports programs, Rory's heart is always with those who need it.

Through all the ups and downs, one thing remained constant: the McIlroy family's unwavering belief in each other. They shared laughter, tears, and dreams, all while navigating the journey together. This bond not only helped Rory become a great golfer but also a great person.

Rory's story teaches us that while talent is important, it's the love and support of family that truly shapes us. So the next time you see someone chasing their dreams, remember the team behind them. Just like Rory, we all have people who cheer us on, whether it's our parents, siblings, or friends. And when we embrace that support, there's no limit to what we can achieve!

In the end, Rory McIlroy's success isn't just his own; it's a family victory—a testament to the power of love, encouragement, and teamwork.

CHAPTER 4

Growing Up Big Dreams: Rory's Path to Greatness

Every dream starts somewhere, and for Rory McIlroy, that journey began in the charming town of Holywood, Northern Ireland. As a young boy, Rory had big dreams of becoming a professional golfer. He was determined to make those dreams a reality, and his journey would take him through challenges, victories, and valuable lessons.

From a very young age, Rory stood out on the golf course. He wasn't just another kid swinging a club; he had a unique passion and talent that set him apart. While other kids played games or watched cartoons, Rory spent his afternoons practicing his swings. He wanted to perfect his technique and learn everything he could about the game. The local golf course became his second home, where he practiced tirelessly, imagining himself playing in front of thousands of fans one day.

Rory's early dedication paid off. By the time he was in his early teens, he was already winning local tournaments and gaining recognition. Picture him standing on the tee, nerves tingling with excitement, as he took his first swing in front of friends and family. With each tournament, Rory learned more about competition, the thrill of victory, and the importance of sportsmanship. Winning felt amazing, but Rory also understood that losing was a part of the game. It taught him resilience and pushed him to keep improving.

As Rory continued to grow, his dreams expanded. He started to envision himself on the world stage, competing against the best golfers in the world. This was no easy feat, but Rory never shied away from hard work. He knew that to reach his goals, he had to put in the effort. He practiced day in and day out, often joining local competitions to sharpen his skills.

One of the most significant moments in Rory's early career came when he turned 15. He earned a spot on the Irish national team, a dream come true for any young golfer. Being part of this team meant he could compete at a higher level, playing against other talented players from around the country. Imagine the pride he felt as he wore the green jersey, representing his country! This experience taught him about teamwork, camaraderie, and the importance of supporting each other.

Rory faced many challenges along the way. There were times when he felt overwhelmed or doubted his abilities. Like any dreamer, he had moments of frustration. Sometimes the ball didn't go where he wanted, or he would struggle in tournaments. During these times, his family and coaches were there to lift his spirits, reminding him that every great athlete experiences ups and downs. They encouraged him to keep believing in himself, reinforcing the idea that perseverance was key.

As he entered his teenage years, Rory began to make a name for himself in the world of golf. His talent was undeniable, and word spread quickly about the young golfer from Holywood. By the age of 16, he became the youngest player to win the prestigious European Amateur Championship. Imagine the joy of achieving such a significant milestone at such a young age! This victory boosted his confidence and motivated him to aim even higher.

Rory's success caught the attention of sponsors and professional golfers. He received offers and opportunities that many young athletes only dream of. But with great opportunities came greater responsibilities. Rory knew he had to stay focused and committed to his goals. He balanced his training with schoolwork, understanding that education was just as important as his golf career.

In 2007, Rory decided to turn professional at just 18 years old. It was a bold move, but he felt ready to take on the challenge. With the support of his family and coaches, he embraced this new chapter in his life. It was the beginning of a thrilling adventure filled with competition, learning, and growth.

As a professional golfer, Rory faced the pressures of the sport. Competing against established players was daunting, but he approached each tournament with enthusiasm and determination. He remembered all the hard work he had put in to get there and used that as motivation. Each swing, each putt, and each moment on the course became a stepping stone toward his dreams.

One of the essential lessons Rory learned during this time was the importance of staying true to himself. As he gained fame, he remained humble and grounded. He often spoke about how he wanted to inspire young golfers, just like he had been inspired. Rory knew that dreams are powerful, but they require dedication and the willingness to overcome obstacles.

With each tournament, Rory grew stronger, both as a golfer and as a person. He celebrated his victories with gratitude, always remembering the people who had helped him along the way. He understood that reaching greatness wasn't just about personal success; it was about uplifting others and making a positive impact.

As Rory McIlroy's journey unfolded, it became clear that his dreams were within reach. His story serves as a reminder to all kids with big dreams: no matter where you start, with passion, perseverance, and support from loved ones, you can achieve greatness. Rory's path to success was filled with determination, hard work, and unwavering belief in himself.

So, whether your dream is to be a golfer, an artist, or anything in between, remember that every step you take brings you closer to your goals. With a heart full of dreams and a spirit ready to soar, you can carve your own path to greatness, just like Rory did!

CHAPTER 5

The Big Win: Rory's First Major Championship Victory

In the world of golf, few moments are as thrilling as winning a major championship. For Rory McIlroy, that moment came on a sunny day in June 2011 at the U.S. Open, a tournament that would change his life forever. Picture this: thousands of fans packed the course at Congressional Country Club in Bethesda, Maryland, their excitement buzzing in the air as they awaited the young golfer's performance.

Rory had been preparing for this tournament for weeks. He trained hard, practiced his swings, and visualized the victory he so desperately wanted. Although he had already made a name for himself, this was his chance to prove that he could compete with the best in the world. As he walked onto the course, he could feel the energy of the crowd. Some were cheering for him, while others were rooting for different players, but all eyes were on the young man from Northern Ireland.

From the very first hole, Rory played with confidence and determination. He had spent countless hours practicing his putting and driving, and now it was time to show what he could do. As he swung his club, the ball flew off like a rocket, landing perfectly on the fairway. With each shot, Rory gained momentum, and the cheers from the crowd grew louder. It was as if the whole world was watching him, and he thrived under the pressure.

Throughout the tournament, Rory faced challenges, just like any athlete does. There were moments when the course tested his skills, with tricky holes and unpredictable weather. But instead of letting pressure get to him, Rory focused on his game. He remembered his family's support, the hours of practice, and all the dreams he had as a kid.

This was his moment, and he was determined to seize it.

As the rounds progressed, Rory's lead over the competition continued to grow. By the final day, he had a comfortable advantage, but he knew that the last round would be the toughest. Imagine the nerves he felt standing on that first tee, knowing he was just 18 holes away from making history. With his heart racing, he took a deep breath and swung his club once more.

The day unfolded beautifully for Rory. He played with precision and grace, showcasing his talent to the world. With each hole, he moved closer to victory. The cheers from the crowd fueled his energy, pushing him to play even better. It was a dream come true, and Rory was living it.

By the time Rory reached the 18th hole, the excitement was palpable. He stood on the edge, knowing that with one final putt, he could secure his place in golf history. The crowd fell silent, all eyes on him. Rory felt a mix of emotions—nervousness, excitement, and an overwhelming sense of joy. He had worked so hard for this moment.

With a steady hand, he lined up his shot. He remembered all the practice sessions, the support from his family, and the dreams he had nurtured since he was a boy. Taking a deep breath, he putted the ball. Time seemed to stand still as it rolled toward the hole.

Then, with a satisfying "plop," the ball dropped in, and the crowd erupted into cheers! Rory had done it—he had won his first major championship!

The moment was magical. Rory raised his arms in triumph, a huge smile spread across his face, and he could hardly believe what had just happened. The feeling of joy and accomplishment washed over him like a wave. He had achieved something that many golfers only dream of, and he had done it at such a young age. It was a testament to his hard work, dedication, and unwavering belief in himself.

As Rory walked off the green, he was greeted by family and friends who had come to support him. Their hugs and congratulations made the victory even sweeter. Rory knew that this win was not just about him; it was about everyone who had been a part of his journey. They had all played a role in helping him reach this incredible milestone.

The victory at the U.S. Open not only earned Rory the coveted trophy but also catapulted him into the spotlight. Suddenly, he was one of the most talked-about players in the world of golf. He received interviews, sponsorship deals, and invitations to play in more prestigious tournaments. But through it all, he remained humble and focused, remembering that his love for the game was what mattered most.

Rory's first major win inspired countless young golfers around the world. He became a role model, proving that with hard work, dreams can come true. His story resonated with kids who were just starting their journeys, showing them that no dream is too big if you are willing to put in the effort.

After the victory, Rory continued to build on his success. He knew that winning was just the beginning; he had to keep pushing himself to grow as a player. With each tournament he entered, he aimed to improve his skills and inspire others along the way. Rory's journey had only just begun, but he was ready for whatever challenges lay ahead.

As we reflect on Rory McIlroy's first major championship victory, it's clear that this moment was a turning point in his career. It was a day filled with joy, determination, and the realization that dreams do come true. For every child watching him that day, Rory became proof that with passion, perseverance, and a little bit of courage, anything is possible. So, let his story inspire you to chase your dreams, no matter how big they may seem!

CHAPTER 6

Words of Wisdom: Inspiring Quotes from Rory McIlroy

Rory McIlroy is not just a superstar golfer; he's also a source of inspiration for many young people around the world. Throughout his career, he has shared powerful quotes that offer guidance and encouragement. In this chapter, we'll explore some of Rory's most memorable sayings and the important lessons they teach us.

One of Rory's famous quotes is, "The more I practice, the luckier I get." This simple yet profound statement highlights the importance of hard work. Rory started playing golf as a child and dedicated countless hours to practicing his swings and putting. He learned early on that success isn't just about talent; it's also about the effort you put in. This lesson is valuable for kids in any field, whether you're practicing sports, music, or studying for school. The more you practice, the better you'll become!

Another quote that stands out is, "I love playing in front of people. It's what I've always dreamed of." This reflects Rory's passion for golf and his love for competition. It teaches us that following our dreams is essential. Rory's journey shows that when you pursue what you love, you find joy and fulfillment. So, if you have a dream—whether it's to be an artist, a scientist, or a professional athlete—don't hesitate to chase it. Your passion can lead to incredible experiences!

Rory has faced his share of challenges throughout his career. He once said, "Every time I've had a setback, I've come back stronger." This quote is a powerful reminder that setbacks are a natural part of life. Everyone encounters obstacles, but how we respond to them makes a difference. Rory teaches us that failure isn't the end; it's an opportunity to learn and grow. If you ever feel discouraged, remember that challenges can help you become more resilient and determined.

Another meaningful quote from Rory is, "You have to be true to yourself." In a world where it's easy to compare ourselves to others, this statement is crucial. Rory emphasizes the importance of being authentic and embracing who you are. It's okay to be different! Each person has unique talents and perspectives. By staying true to yourself, you can shine in your own way and contribute something special to the world.

Rory also values teamwork and support. He once mentioned, "Golf is a game where you can always improve, and it's important to surround yourself with people who want to help you." This quote highlights the importance of having a strong support system. No one achieves greatness alone; we all need friends, family, and mentors to guide us along the way. So, whether it's on the golf course or in everyday life, remember that teamwork and collaboration can lead to amazing achievements.

In another inspiring moment, Rory said, "The only limits you have are the limits you believe." This powerful statement encourages kids to think beyond boundaries. Often, we set limitations for ourselves based on fear or doubt. Rory reminds us that if we believe in our abilities, we can accomplish incredible things. So, dream big and don't let anyone tell you that you can't achieve your goals!

Rory also emphasizes gratitude in his life. He often expresses thankfulness for his opportunities and experiences. One of his quotes states, "I'm very grateful for everything I've achieved, and I want to give back." This mindset teaches us that success isn't just about personal accomplishments; it's also about helping others. Whether it's volunteering, mentoring, or simply being kind, giving back can create a positive impact in the world.

Moreover, Rory believes in the importance of enjoying the journey. He once said, "At the end of the day, I just want to have fun and enjoy what I do." This quote serves as a reminder that while achieving our goals is essential, enjoying the process is equally important. Whether you're competing in a sport or working on a project, find joy in what you do. It makes the journey much more rewarding!

As we reflect on Rory's words, let's carry these lessons with us. His quotes remind us of the values of hard work, authenticity, resilience, and gratitude. By embracing these principles, we can all create our paths to success and inspire those around us.

Rory McIlroy's journey is filled with wisdom and motivation. His quotes not only inspire young golfers but anyone striving to reach their dreams. They teach us that with determination, passion, and a positive attitude, anything is possible. So, as you embark on your own adventures, remember to hold on to these words of wisdom. Let them guide you, inspire you, and remind you that you have the power to achieve great things!

In conclusion, Rory's inspirational quotes encourage us to pursue our passions, overcome challenges, and remain true to ourselves. By incorporating these lessons into our lives, we can not only reach our goals but also inspire others to do the same. So, dream big, work hard, and enjoy every moment of the journey!

CHAPTER 7

Golf Fun: Rory's Best Tips and Tricks for Young Players

Golf can be an exciting and rewarding sport, and no one knows this better than Rory McIlroy! As one of the best golfers in the world, Rory has learned a lot over the years and is eager to share his favorite tips and tricks with young players like you. Whether you're just starting out or looking to improve your game, these fun insights can help you become a better golfer while having a blast on the course.

1. Practice Makes Perfect

First and foremost, Rory emphasizes the importance of practice. He often says, "The more I practice, the luckier I get." This means that the more time you spend practicing your swings, putting, and chipping, the better you'll become! Set aside time each week to work on your skills. It could be as simple as hitting balls at the driving range or putting on your living room carpet. The key is consistency—regular practice will lead to improvement!

2. Have Fun with Friends

Golf is not just about competition; it's also about having fun! Rory encourages young golfers to play with friends and family. Organizing friendly games can make practice more enjoyable. You can set up fun challenges, like who can make the longest putt or who can hit the ball closest to the hole. Enjoying the game with others creates great memories and keeps the spirit of fun alive!

3. Focus on Your Grip

One of the first things Rory teaches is how to hold the golf club correctly. A proper grip is essential for making solid contact with the ball. Hold the club with your fingers, not your palms, and make sure your grip is firm but relaxed. Rory often emphasizes that a good grip leads to better control of your shots. Practice gripping the club until it feels comfortable, and you'll see improvements in your swings!

4. Stance and Posture Matter

Your stance and posture play a significant role in your performance. Rory suggests that young players stand with their feet shoulder-width apart and bend slightly at the knees. This balanced position helps you stay stable while swinging. Remember to keep your back straight and your head still during the swing. Good posture will lead to more accurate shots and a smoother swing!

5. Take Your Time

Rory believes that patience is crucial in golf. Rushing your shots can lead to mistakes. When you're about to hit the ball, take a deep breath, visualize your shot, and focus. Rory often takes a moment to gather his thoughts before each swing. This practice helps calm his nerves and leads to better shots. So, next time you're on the course, remember to take your time!

6. Learn the Short Game

While long drives can be exciting, Rory emphasizes the importance of the short game—putting and chipping around the greens. These shots can make a big difference in your score! Spend time practicing your putting and learn different techniques for chipping. Try different clubs and find what works best for you. Rory believes that mastering the short game can lower your scores and make you a more well-rounded player.

7. Play Smart

Golf is a mental game as much as it is physical. Rory advises young golfers to think strategically about each shot. Consider the layout of the course, the wind, and the condition of the greens. Sometimes it's better to play safe rather than trying to hit every shot perfectly. Rory often chooses to play conservatively when needed. This approach can lead to fewer mistakes and better overall scores.

8. Stay Positive

A positive attitude can change everything! Rory often talks about the importance of staying upbeat, even when things don't go as planned. If you miss a shot, don't get discouraged. Instead, focus on what you can learn from the experience. Golf is about progress, and every golfer, even the best, has off days. Embracing a positive mindset will help you enjoy the game more and build resilience.

9. Watch the Pros

One of the best ways to learn is by watching professionals play. Rory suggests tuning in to golf tournaments on TV or visiting local courses to watch pro golfers. Pay attention to their techniques, how they handle different situations, and their strategies. You can pick up valuable tips just by observing how they play!

10. Celebrate Your Progress

Finally, Rory encourages young golfers to celebrate their achievements, no matter how small. Whether you hit a great drive, sink a long putt, or simply enjoy a day on the course with friends, take time to appreciate your progress. Keep track of your improvements, and don't be afraid to share your successes with others. Celebrating progress keeps you motivated and excited about the game.

Conclusion

Golf is a fantastic sport that combines skill, strategy, and fun. Rory McIlroy's tips and tricks can help you enjoy the game while becoming a better golfer. Remember to practice regularly, play with friends, stay positive, and most importantly, have fun! With dedication and the right mindset, you can follow in Rory's footsteps and create your own exciting journey in the world of golf. So grab your clubs, hit the course, and enjoy every moment on your golfing adventure!

CHAPTER 8

Around the Globe: Rory's Adventures on the Golf Course

Rory McIlroy isn't just a phenomenal golfer; he's also an adventurer who has traveled the world, playing golf in some of the most exciting places. In this chapter, we'll take a journey with Rory to discover the incredible courses he's played, the cultures he's experienced, and the memories he's made along the way.

Tee Time in the U.S.A.

One of Rory's favorite places to play is in the United States, particularly during the famous PGA Tour. The vibrant atmosphere of the tournaments, filled with cheering fans and stunning landscapes, makes each event unforgettable. One of his most notable adventures took place at the iconic Augusta National Golf Club, home of the Masters Tournament. Rory has always dreamed of winning at Augusta, and he's played there multiple times, feeling the excitement in the air as he competes against the best players in the world. The beautiful azaleas and towering pines create a magical setting, and Rory often shares how inspiring it is to walk those fairways.

The Links of Scotland

Rory's roots trace back to Ireland, but he loves playing in Scotland, where golf began. The Scottish courses are unique, with rolling hills and unpredictable weather. One of Rory's memorable experiences was at St Andrews, known as the "Home of Golf." The course is famous for its history, having been played for over 600 years! Rory has talked about the thrill of standing on the first tee at St Andrews, knowing that many legendary golfers have walked the same path. The charm of playing on such a historic course adds to his love for the game.

Adventure Down Under

Rory's adventures also took him to Australia, where he played in the Australian Open. The breathtaking views of the ocean and vibrant wildlife made this trip unforgettable. Rory enjoys playing in different conditions, and the Australian courses challenge him with their sandy beaches and coastal winds. He has often said that each round in Australia is an adventure in itself, with the beauty of nature surrounding him as he plays. The warmth of the Australian people and their love for golf adds to the experience, making it feel like a big family reunion.

Competing in Asia

Traveling to Asia has also been a highlight of Rory's career. He's participated in tournaments in countries like China and South Korea, where the culture is rich and vibrant. Rory loves exploring local cuisines, meeting fans, and learning about traditions. In China, he played at the prestigious Mission Hills Golf Club, where he enjoyed both the challenging course and the stunning landscapes. Each visit allows him to connect with young golfers and inspire them to chase their dreams, just as he did.

The Majestic Courses of Europe

Rory has also played in various European countries, from France to Italy. Each place offers unique challenges and breathtaking scenery. At the French Open, Rory enjoyed the beautiful countryside and the enthusiastic crowds that filled the stands. In Italy, the stunning architecture and delicious food made his visit even more special. He often shares stories of his adventures, from trying new dishes to exploring historic sites, showing how golf can bring people together across different cultures.

A Chance to Give Back

Rory's travels aren't just about playing golf; they also provide opportunities to give back. He has participated in charity events worldwide, using his platform to support important causes. Rory believes in making a difference in the communities he visits. For example, during one of his tournaments in the U.S., he helped raise funds for youth golf programs. Rory enjoys inspiring kids to play golf, and he often visits schools to talk about the sport and its values. His commitment to giving back shows that golf is more than just a game; it's a way to connect and create positive change.

Making Lifelong Friends

Throughout his travels, Rory has made friends from all corners of the globe. Meeting other golfers, fans, and people who love the game adds a special touch to his adventures. Rory often reflects on how these friendships have enriched his life. He believes that golf is about community, and he cherishes the connections he has made. Whether he's playing a round with fellow pros or sharing a laugh with young fans, these moments make his journey even more meaningful.

Conclusion: The Joy of Golfing Adventures

Rory McIlroy's adventures around the globe showcase the beauty and excitement of golf. From the historic courses in Scotland to the vibrant tournaments in the U.S. and the scenic landscapes in Australia, each experience has shaped him as a player and as a person. Through his travels, Rory not only hones his skills but also learns valuable lessons about different cultures, friendships, and the joy of giving back.

As young golfers, you too can dream of exploring the world through golf. Who knows? One day you might find yourself on a beautiful course, making memories just like Rory. So grab your clubs, embrace the adventure, and let the game take you places you've always dreamed of!

CHAPTER 9

Facing Challenges: Rory's Comebacks and Valuable Lessons

Every great athlete faces challenges, and Rory McIlroy is no exception. His journey in golf has been filled with ups and downs, but what sets him apart is his incredible ability to overcome obstacles and learn from them. In this chapter, we'll explore some of the tough moments Rory has faced, how he turned them into valuable lessons, and how his story can inspire you.

The Road to Recovery

One of the biggest challenges Rory faced occurred in 2015 when he injured his ankle while playing soccer with friends. This injury forced him to miss several important tournaments, including the Open Championship. For a golfer, this was a tough blow, and Rory felt the disappointment deeply. However, instead of letting the injury hold him back, he used this time to focus on his recovery and improve his mental game.

Rory learned that taking a break doesn't mean giving up. He spent his recovery time studying the game, watching videos of past tournaments, and visualizing himself playing again. This experience taught him the importance of patience and resilience. Sometimes, stepping back can help you come back stronger!

Dealing with Pressure

Another significant challenge for Rory came during the 2011 Masters Tournament. After an excellent start, he found himself leading the competition. But as the final round approached, the pressure began to build. Rory struggled on the back nine, ultimately finishing in fourth place. It was a heartbreaking moment for him, especially because he was so close to winning.

However, Rory took this setback as a learning opportunity. He reflected on what went wrong and realized he needed to manage pressure better. He began practicing mindfulness and breathing techniques to help stay calm in high-stress situations. This experience taught him that it's okay to feel nervous, but how you respond to that pressure can make all the difference.

Embracing Setbacks

Throughout his career, Rory has faced setbacks in various tournaments. After his disappointing finish at the Masters in 2011, he experienced another setback at the 2013 Open Championship. Despite feeling ready to win, he didn't perform as expected. Instead of letting frustration take over, Rory embraced the lesson that golf is unpredictable.

He learned that even the best players have bad days. This realization helped him to be kinder to himself and focus on the bigger picture. Rory began to see setbacks as stepping stones rather than roadblocks. This change in perspective allowed him to approach the game with more positivity and determination.

The Importance of Support

Rory has always credited his family and friends for their unwavering support during tough times. Whether it's his parents who encouraged him to pursue his passion or his close friends who cheered him on, their belief in him has been a vital part of his journey. When faced with challenges, Rory leans on this support network, reminding himself that he's not alone.

This teaches young players the importance of surrounding themselves with positive influences. Having friends and family who believe in you can provide strength and motivation during difficult moments. Rory's story is a reminder that teamwork doesn't just happen on the golf course—it's also about the people who lift you up when you need it most.

Finding the Silver Lining

Rory believes that every challenge brings an opportunity to grow. After each setback, he takes time to reflect on what he can learn. This practice helps him understand that failures are not the end but rather a chance to improve. He often says, "The only way to succeed is to keep trying." This mindset encourages him to keep pushing forward, no matter the obstacles in his path.

For young golfers, this lesson is crucial. When faced with challenges in sports or life, remember that it's okay to stumble. What matters is how you respond. Embrace the learning process, stay determined, and keep striving for your goals.

Conclusion: Rising Above Challenges

Rory McIlroy's journey is filled with challenges, but each one has shaped him into the golfer he is today. His ability to face setbacks with grace and determination is an inspiration for young athletes everywhere. By learning from his experiences, we see that challenges can lead to growth, resilience, and ultimately success.

So, when you find yourself facing a tough moment—whether it's in sports, school, or life—remember Rory's story. Embrace the challenges, lean on your support system, and keep believing in yourself. With hard work and a positive attitude, you too can rise above any obstacle and reach for your dreams!

CHAPTER 10

Dream Big: How You Can Follow in Rory's Footsteps!

Rory McIlroy is more than just a talented golfer; he's a symbol of hard work, determination, and the power of dreams. In this final chapter, we'll explore how you can follow in Rory's footsteps and chase your own big dreams, no matter what they are. Whether you want to be a great golfer, a scientist, an artist, or anything else, the lessons from Rory's journey can inspire you to reach for the stars!

Believe in Yourself

The first step to achieving your dreams is believing in yourself. Rory often talks about how crucial self-confidence is to his success. He faced many challenges, but he always reminded himself that he had the talent and determination to succeed. Just like Rory, you need to trust in your abilities. Write down your goals and believe that you can achieve them. Remember, every champion started as a beginner!

Set Clear Goals

Rory didn't become a superstar overnight; he set specific goals and worked hard to achieve them. Think about what you want to accomplish. Do you want to improve your golf skills? Maybe you want to make the school basketball team or ace your math test. Setting clear, achievable goals gives you a roadmap to follow. Break your big dreams into smaller, manageable steps, and celebrate each achievement along the way!

Practice, Practice, Practice

Hard work is the secret sauce behind success. Rory didn't become a top golfer by sitting on the couch; he practiced relentlessly. Whether it's swinging a golf club, studying for a test, or honing any skill, regular practice is essential. Make a practice schedule and stick to it. You might not see immediate results, but remember, every bit of effort counts! Over time, those small steps will lead to big improvements.

Learn from Mistakes

Everyone makes mistakes, even the best athletes in the world. Rory faced setbacks throughout his career, but instead of being discouraged, he used them as learning opportunities. When you stumble, don't be afraid to evaluate what went wrong and how you can improve. Embrace mistakes as part of the journey! Each lesson learned makes you stronger and wiser.

Stay Positive

A positive attitude can make a world of difference. Rory often talks about the importance of keeping a good mindset, especially during tough times. Surround yourself with positive people who encourage you. When faced with challenges, try to focus on the good and keep moving forward. Remember, a smile can change everything, and staying optimistic helps you see solutions rather than problems.

Find a Mentor

Having someone to guide you can be incredibly helpful. Rory has had coaches and mentors throughout his career who provided valuable advice and support. Look for someone you admire—maybe a coach, a teacher, or even a family member—who can inspire you and share their wisdom. Don't hesitate to ask for help or advice; you might be surprised by how willing people are to support you.

Embrace Teamwork

Rory understands that while individual talent is important, teamwork plays a significant role in success. Whether you're on a sports team, in a classroom, or working on a project, collaborating with others can bring out the best in you. Be open to sharing ideas and learning from your teammates. Supporting each other makes the journey more enjoyable and can lead to greater achievements.

Dream Big, Start Small

Rory's journey began with a dream, but he didn't jump straight to the top. He started small, learning the basics of golf and gradually moving up to compete at higher levels. Similarly, don't be afraid to dream big but start with small, actionable steps. Every great achievement is built on a series of smaller successes. So go ahead and dream big, but take that first small step today!

Give Back

One of the most beautiful lessons Rory teaches us is the importance of giving back. He often participates in charity events and encourages young golfers to help their communities. As you chase your dreams, remember to lift others along the way. Whether it's helping a friend with their homework, volunteering, or simply being kind, giving back creates a positive ripple effect that can inspire others.

Conclusion: Your Journey Awaits

Rory McIlroy's journey shows us that with hard work, determination, and a positive mindset, anything is possible. As you finish this book, remember that your dreams are within reach. Follow in Rory's footsteps by believing in yourself, setting goals, practicing, learning from mistakes, and embracing teamwork. Your journey may be unique, but the principles of chasing dreams remain the same.

So, what are you waiting for? Grab your clubs, your books, or whatever you need, and take that first step towards your dreams. The world is full of opportunities waiting for you, and just like Rory, you can make your mark! Dream big and go for it!

CONCLUSION

Rory's Amazing Journey!

As we wrap up the exciting story of Rory McIlroy, we hope you've enjoyed every swing and every triumph! Rory's journey from a young boy with big dreams to a golf superstar shows us all that anything is possible if you work hard and believe in yourself.

Rory faced challenges, but he never let them stop him. Instead, he learned valuable lessons about perseverance and having fun along the way. Whether he was practicing in his backyard or competing in big tournaments, Rory always kept his passion for golf close to his heart. This is a reminder that it's okay to stumble; what matters is getting back up and trying again!

Now that you know all about Rory's incredible adventures, think about your own dreams. What do you want to achieve? Remember, just like Rory, you can reach for the stars with hard work and a positive attitude.

Thank you for exploring Rory McIlroy's world! Your support means everything to me. If you enjoyed this book, I would be so grateful if you could leave a positive review. Your kind words help spread the magic of Rory's story to other kids who may also want to chase their dreams. Keep dreaming big, and who knows? You might be the next star!

www.ingramcontent.com/pod-product-compliance
Lightning Source LLC
LaVergne TN
LVHW052006020125
800336LV00011B/1078